Meet the Key Workers

HEALTH CARE WORKERS

By Shalini Vallepur

KidHaven Publishing

Published in 2024 by
KidHaven Publishing, an Imprint of Greenhaven Publishing, LLC
2544 Clinton St., Buffalo, NY 14224

This edition is published by arrangement with Booklife Publishing

Written by: Shalini Vallepur
Edited by: John Wood
Designed by: Jasmine Pointer

Cataloging-in-Publication Data

Names: Vallepur, Shalini.
Title: Health care workers / Shalini Vallepur.
Description: New York : KidHaven Publishing, 2024. | Series: Meet the key workers | Includes glossary and index.
Identifiers: ISBN 9781534544512 (pbk) | ISBN 9781534544529 (library bound) | ISBN 9781534544536 (ebook)
Subjects: LCSH: Medical personnel-- Juvenile literature
Classification: LCC R727.5 V35 2024 | DDC 610.69 --dc23

Manufactured in the United States of America

CPSIA compliance information: Batch #CSKH24: For further information contact Greenhaven Publishing LLC at 1-844-317-7404.

Please visit our website, www.greenhavenpublishing.com. For a free color catalog of all our high-quality books, call toll free 1-844-317-7404 or fax 1-844-317-7405.

Find us on

Image Credits

All images are courtesy of Shutterstock.com, unless otherwise specified. With thanks to Getty Images, Thinkstock Photo and iStockphoto.

Cover – Daniel M Ernst, Studio_G, VectorPlotnikoff, Victor Z. 2–3 – fizkes. 4–5 – melhijad, Inspiring, Jenson, aShatilov. 6–7 – worawit_j, Spotmatik Ltd, KK Tan, msr melooo1. 8–9 – Halfpoint, Kamil Macniak, Oksana Kuzmina, DC Studio, Monkey Business Images, Evellean. 10–11 – hedgehog94, Monkey Business Images, Tyler Olson. 12–13 – Bahau, Stanislav71, Silarock, Monkey Business Images. 14–15 – Monkey Business Images, Inspiring, DGLimages, Diego Cervo. 16–17 – Rob Wilson, Monkey Business Images, Pablo Rogat, DEEMKA STUDIO, Elena Pimukova. 18–19 – Olesia Bilkei, Pimonmartj, Rvector. 20–21 – Microgen, Monkey Business Images, Andrew Rybalko, Vitalii Petrenko. 22–23 – wavebreakmedia, CharacterFamily70, elenabsl.

CONTENTS

Words that look like **this** can be found in the glossary on page 24.

HERE TO HELP

There are lots of jobs in the world and each one is different. Some jobs are always needed. The people who do these jobs are called key workers.

Key can sometimes mean needed and important.

Farmers are always needed to grow the food we eat.

Without key workers, we would not have the things we need to live safely, such as food and **services**.

PEOPLE IN

HEALTH CARE

Have you ever visited a doctor or taken **medicine**? Have you ever had a hearing test or been to a dentist? These are just a few services in health care.

A dentist checks your teeth.

We need health care services when we are hurt, ill, or just need a checkup. Lots of people work in health care services to keep us healthy. Let's learn all about them!

IN THE HOSPITAL

There are many key workers in hospitals doing different jobs. Each job is important. If you feel ill, you might visit a GP first. A GP is **trained** to find out what's wrong and can give out **prescriptions**.

Many doctors are trained to care for a certain age group or a certain part of the body.

A bone doctor can look after broken bones.

Some doctors are trained to care for babies and children.

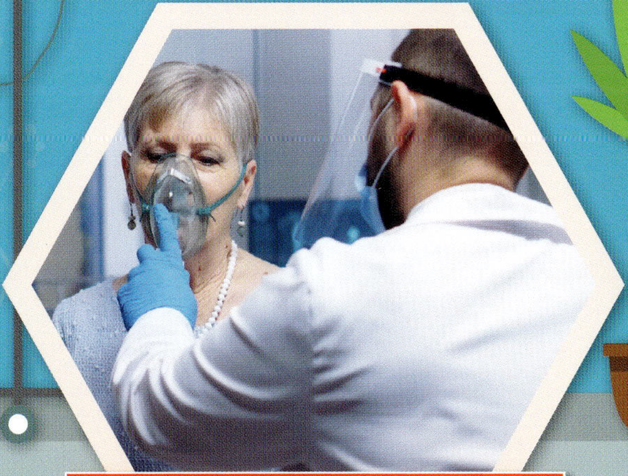

A lung doctor can help with lung **diseases**, such as asthma.

A surgeon is trained to carry out **operations**.

Nurses work alongside doctors to care for **patients**. Nurses take care of patients and may give them medicine, such as **vaccines**. A midwife also works alongside doctors to look after women having a baby.

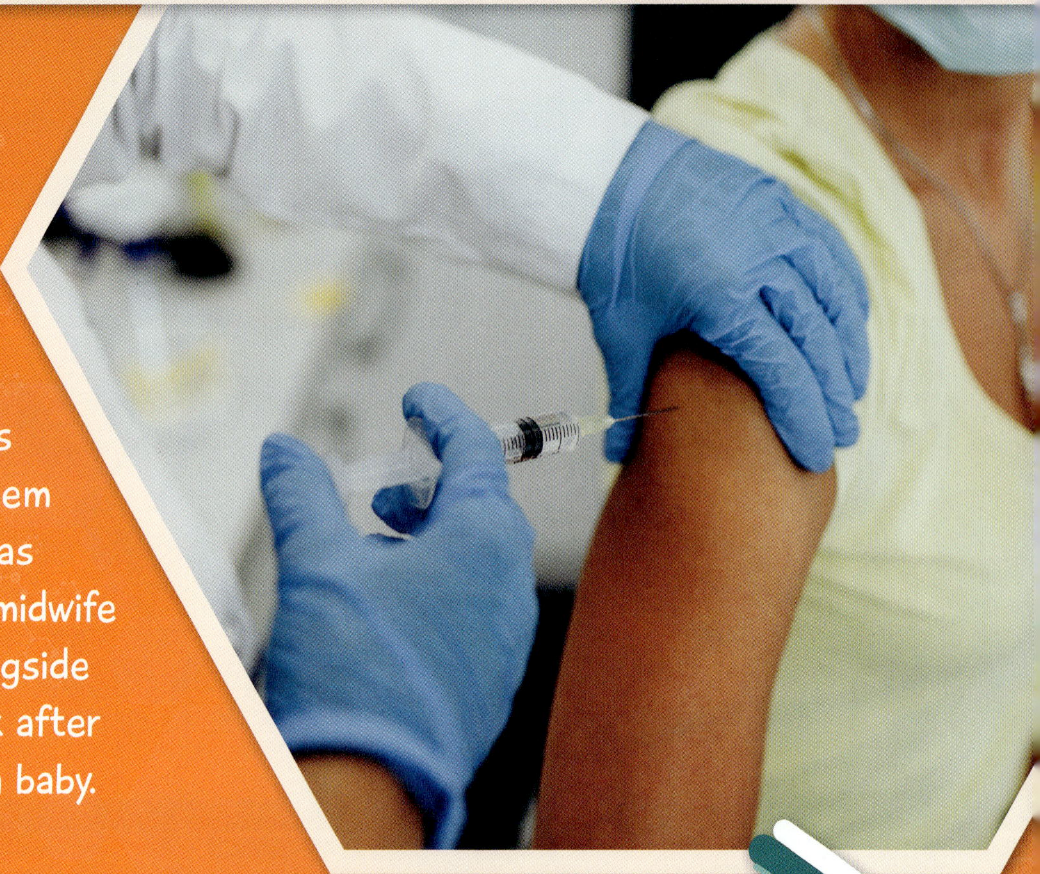

A midwife

Some nurses treat people in their homes.

Support staff do lots of different jobs that help doctors and nurses treat patients. Some are in charge of taking blood from people, while others might be in charge of explaining treatments to people.

Hospitals always need to be kept clean. Cleaners work hard to make sure hospitals are a clean and safe place to be.

Hospital porters deliver important things around hospitals. They take medicine from one place to another and help people get around the hospital.

Hospital porters also bring people food and clean bedsheets.

IN THE

CARE HOME

Some people live in care homes if they are sick or need to be looked after. Care homes are run by care staff, who are always there to help.

Care staff can sometimes include nurses.

Care staff help the people living in care homes with everyday things, such as getting dressed and cooking. Sometimes, care staff sleep at care homes to make sure everybody is safe and well.

AT THE

PHARMACY

Some medicines can be bought at a pharmacy. A pharmacist is in charge of a pharmacy. They may give **advice** to people who are ill and get their medicine ready.

Pharmacy assistants and dispensers work with the pharmacist. They talk to people about medicines and check prescriptions.

Checkups!

We may visit different health care services for checkups. Dentists and dental nurses check inside our mouths. They make sure our teeth and gums are healthy.

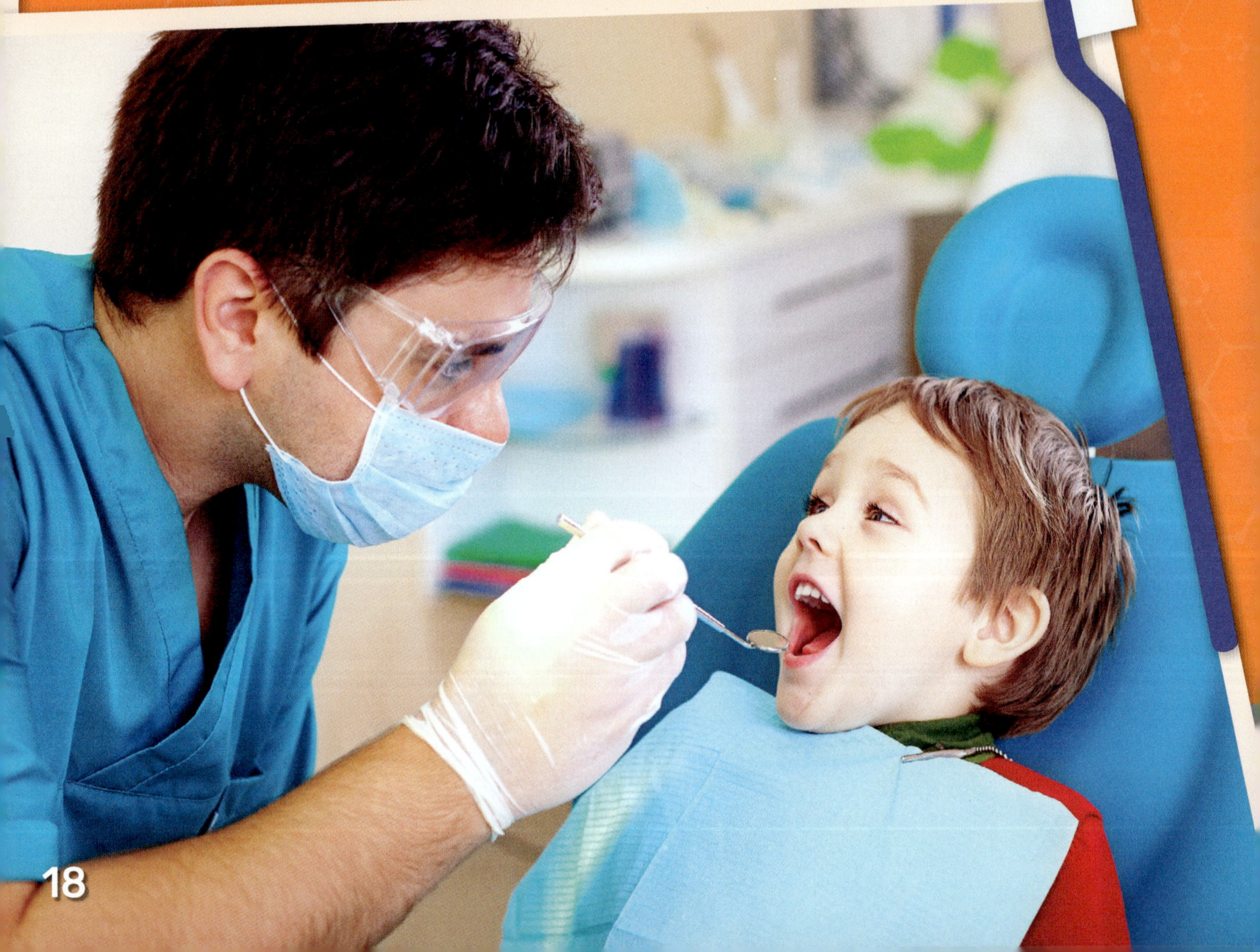

When we go to the optician, an optometrist checks our eyes. If we need glasses, a dispensing optician helps us find the right pair.

HEALTHY MINDS

Looking after our **mental health** is important. A psychiatrist is a doctor who can help treat mental health problems. Psychiatrists prescribe medicine to people who come to them for help.

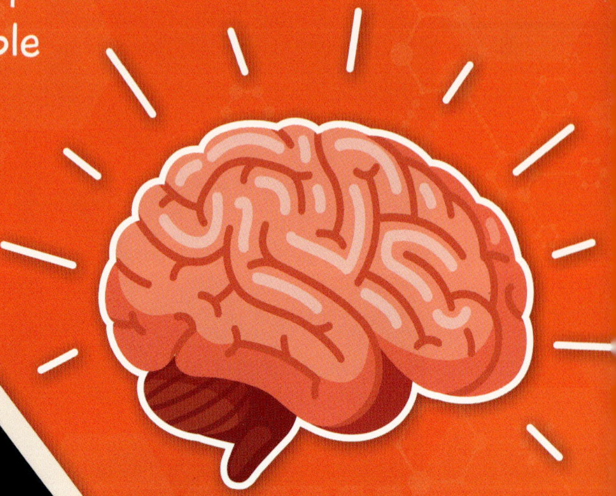

There are lots of mental health services that children can call if they need to. You can ask your teacher about this.

Therapists and counselors can be spoken to on the phone. They listen to people and help them deal with their problems.

KEEPING US

HEALTHY

So many people work extremely hard to make sure we are healthy and well. The next time you use a health care service, don't forget to say thank you!

Now you know about some of the people who work in health care! Can you match each job below with the right person?

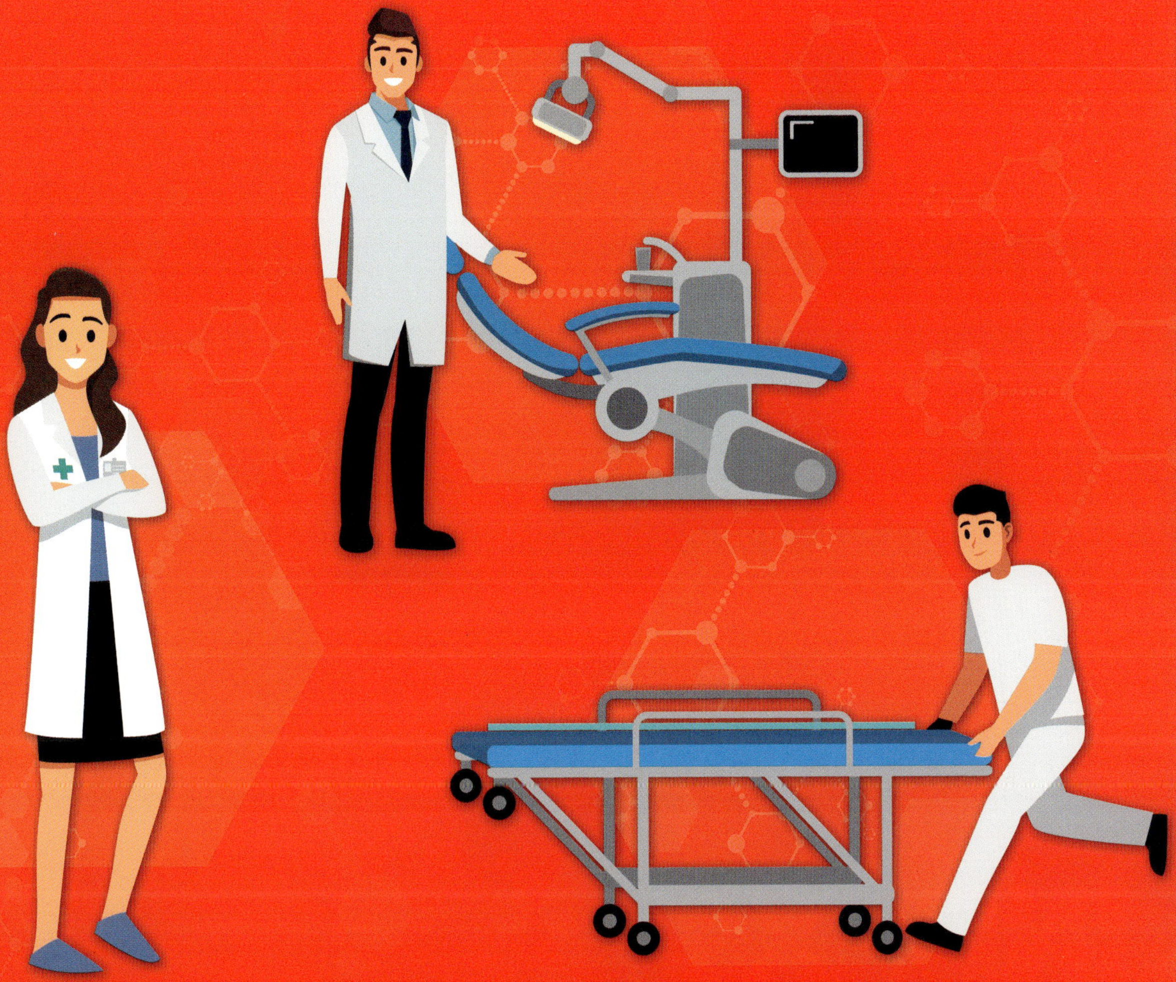

Hospital porter	Pharmacy assistant	Dentist
Delivers things around the hospital	Checks prescriptions and talks to customers	Checks our teeth and gums

GLOSSARY

advice	something that is said to help someone decide what to do next
diseases	problems with the body that make us feel unwell
medicine	something used or taken to fight off diseases
mental health	how healthy and well we feel in our minds
operations	events where special doctors open up someone's body to fix a problem using special tools
patients	ill people who visit a doctor or hospital
prescriptions	information about what medicine a person needs
services	tasks or actions that people pay other people to do, such as caring for older people, fixing things that are broken, or cleaning
trained	having been taught how to do a job
vaccines	a type of medicine that stops us getting ill from certain diseases

INDEX